Junior Science
light and dark

Terry Jennings

Illustrations by David Anstey

Gloucester Press
New York · London · Toronto · Sydney

About this book

You can learn many things about light and dark from this book. It tells you about the ways in which light and dark affect different things. There are lots of activities and experiments for you to try. You can find out which animals and plants respond to light and dark, and much more.

First published in the United States in 1991 by Gloucester Press 387 Park Avenue South New York, NY 10016

© Mirabel Books Limited 1990

This book was designed and produced by Mirabel Books Limited

Library of Congress Cataloging-in-Publication Data

Jennings, Terry J.
    Light and dark / Terry Jennings.
        p. cm. -- (Junior science)
    Includes index.
    Summary: Explores the differences between light and dark covering such topics as shadows, nocturnal animals, how plants use light, and reflection of light.
    ISBN 0-531-17277-5
    1. Light--Juvenile literature. 2. Shades and shadows--Juvenile literature. [1. Light. 2. Shadows.] I. Title. II. Series: Jennings, Terry J. Junior science.
    QC360.J463   1991
    535--dc20

90-44678   CIP   AC

These are two pictures of the same scene. In the left one it is light, and you can see lots of things. In the other picture it is dark and you cannot see as much.

sunrise

The Sun provides the light that lets us see things in the daytime. The day starts to get lighter and lighter when the Sun appears. This is called sunrise. The Sun rises in the east.

sunset

The sky then gets lighter and lighter until noon,
and then very gradually, it gets darker
until sunset. The Sun sets in the west.
After that it is nighttime and dark.

People cannot see things easily in the dark. You can play a game to find out what happens when you cannot see things. Put on a blindfold and get a friend to put some things on a table. You have to say what they are by picking up the things and feeling them. You will discover that it is much easier to tell what things are by seeing them rather than feeling them.

The light from the Sun can make things cast shadows. The shadows form behind things that the Sun's light cannot pass through. You can make a life-size cutout of somebody using a shadow. Get a friend to stand in sunlight at the edge of a large piece of paper. Then draw around your friend's shadow and cut out the shape with scissors.

As the Sun moves across the sky, shadows also move. You can show this by pushing a stick in a pot of soil, putting it out in the sunlight and marking the position of the stick's shadow on the ground. An hour later the shadow will have moved. An hour later still it will have moved again – every hour it is in a different place. Notice also that the shadow is longest near the beginning and end of the day, and shortest near noon.

9

Any light will cast shadows, not just the Sun. For example, a flashlight will make shadows. Get somebody to shine a flashlight on a wall in a dark room. You can make shapes with your hands to form shadow pictures on the wall. Or you can cut shapes out of cardboard and tape them to sticks. You can then use the shapes to give a shadow puppet show.

Things that easily let light pass through them are called transparent. The glass in a window is transparent and you can see things through it. Other things, such as colored plastic bags, let light pass but you cannot see things clearly through them. These are called translucent. And still other things do not let any light through at all, and these are called opaque.

A piece of wood or metal is opaque.
Collect various things and hold
them up to the light. Note which
ones are transparent or translucent,
and which are opaque.

Translucent things

Opaque things

Transparent things

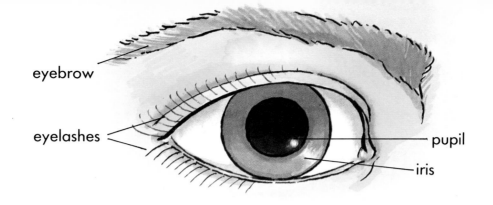

eyebrow

eyelashes

pupil

iris

We see with our eyes, which react to light that enters them. Light goes into the eye through a small hole called the pupil. If you look out a bright window the pupil is small, so that too much light does not enter the eye.

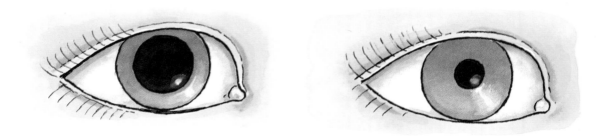

But if you look into a dark closet, the pupil becomes large to let in as much light as possible.

14

You cannot always believe your eyes. Here are some puzzle pictures.

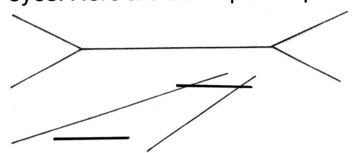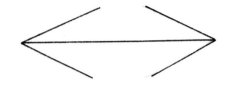

The pair of horizontal lines are of the same length. And although the red lines look curved, they are really straight.

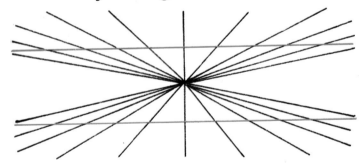

The picture on the right can look like a young girl with a feathery hat. Or it can seem like an old woman with a big nose and pointed chin.

15

Some animals like the dark and come out only at night to feed. They include most owls and moths. Mice, wood lice, slugs and snails are also active at night. Other animals like the light and can be seen during the day. They include butterflies, bees, wasps and most kinds of birds. By looking around your backyard, or a park, you can make a list of the two types of animals. Note which ones are around in daylight. Then look under stones and pieces of

wasp

bee

sparrow

wood to find animals that are hidden away. These are the ones that like the dark.

Animals that like the light

Animals that like the dark

snail

slug

woodlouse

moth

17

Plants need light to grow. You can prove this with an experiment. Take two plastic pots (paint faces on them if you want) and fill them with moist cotton. Put some orange pits on the cotton, and put one pot near a sunny window and the other in a dark closet. The orange pits will grow, but look different in each pot. Seedlings in the light will be shorter but with bright green leaves.

Seeds grown in the dark will make taller plants, but they will be weak and pale.

This shows that light is needed to make plants strong and healthy. Things look shiny when light bounces off them – when they reflect light. Some things are more shiny than others. Polished metal, for example, is shinier than polished wood. A mirror reflects light well. You can use a mirror to reflect a patch of sunlight onto a wall. The Moon also reflects light. It does not give off light of its own, but reflects light from the Sun.

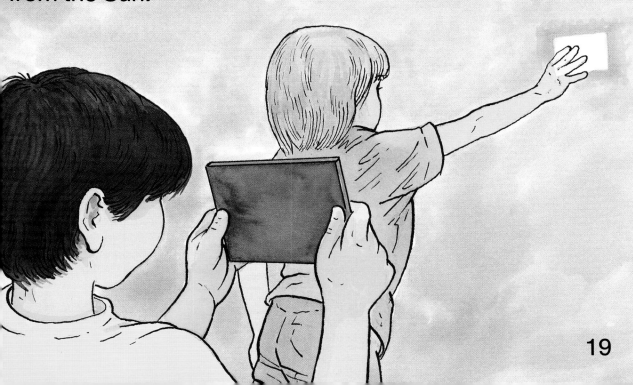

Mirrors turn things around. We say they form a mirror image. A boy looked into a mirror and winked his right eye, but his reflection winked its left eye. He touched his right ear, but the reflection in the mirror touched its left ear. His name was Ricky and he wrote it on a piece of paper. When he held the paper up to the mirror, its reflection showed the letters reversed. You can also make a shiny tin can or the back of a spoon act like curved mirrors. Reflections that appear in these kinds of mirrors are bent or even upside-down.

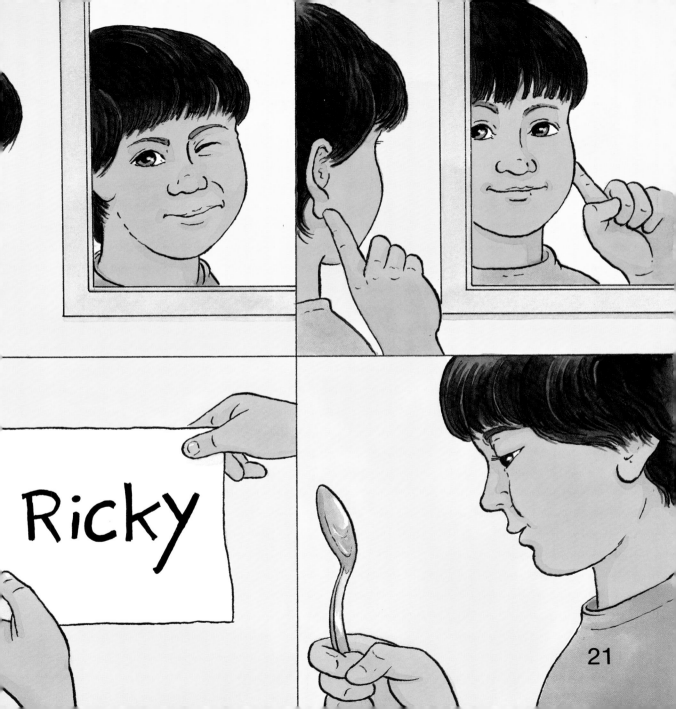

Ricky

21

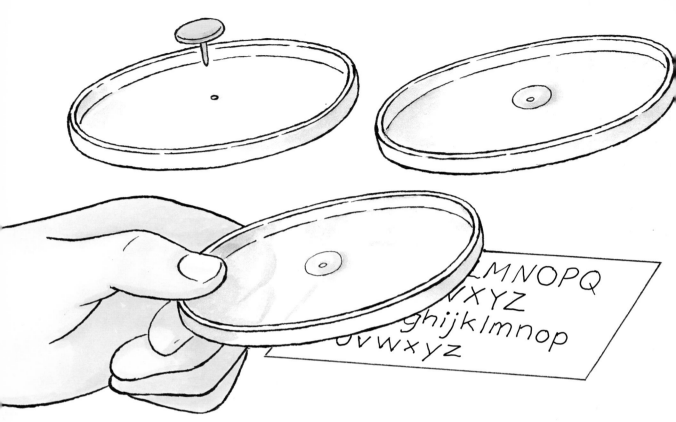

A magnifying glass is a type of lens. But a lens does not have to be made of glass – you can even make one out of water. Find a clear plastic lid and make a hole in the center with a thumbtack. Put a drop of water in the hole and hold your watery lens over some writing. The writing will look bigger.

glossary

Here are the meanings of some words that you might have met for the first time in reading this book.

dark: with no light, or with very little light.

lens: a piece of glass or clear plastic with a slightly curved surface. Some lenses magnify or make things look bigger.

light: the opposite of dark. Light makes it possible to see things.

magnifying glass: a lens or group of lenses that makes things look larger.

opaque: not letting light through.

sunrise: dawn, the time when the Sun begins to rise in the eastern sky.

sunset: when the Sun goes down in the west just before night.

translucent: letting light through but not well enough to see clearly through.

transparent: letting light through and clear enough to see through.

23

Index

PRINTED IN BELGIUM BY
proost
INTERNATIONAL BOOK PRODUCTION